Meadow Muffins

Cowboy Rhymes and Other B.S.

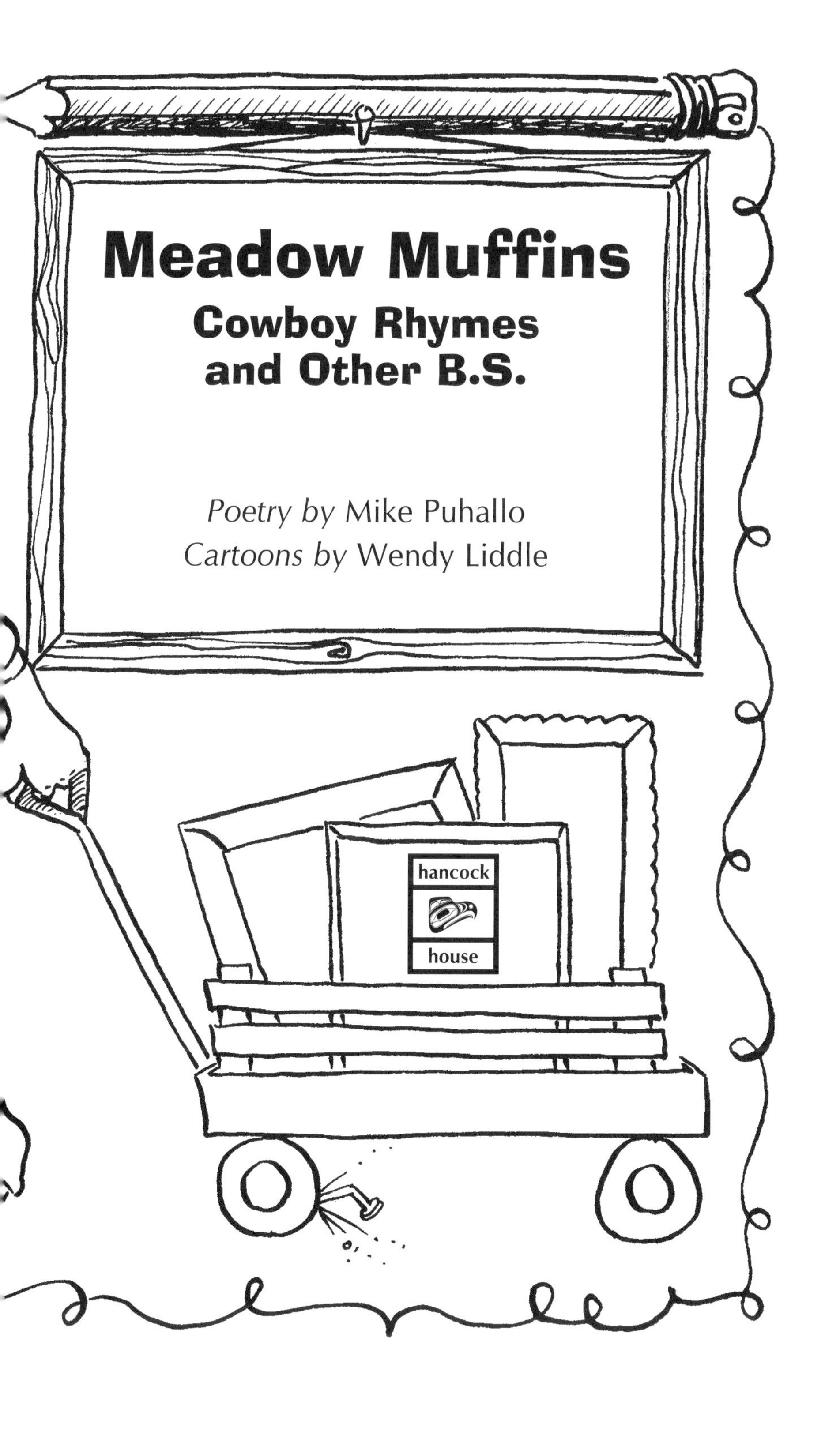

Meadow Muffins

Cowboy Rhymes and Other B.S.

Poetry by Mike Puhallo
Cartoons by Wendy Liddle

hancock house

ISBN 0-88839-436-5

Cataloging in Publication Data
Puhallo, Mike, 1953-
Meadow muffins

ISBN 0-88839-436-5

1. Cowboys—Poetry. I. Liddle, Wendy. II. Title.
PS8581.U42M42 1999 C811'.54 C98-911164-4
PR9199.3.P77M42 1999

Printed in Canada—Kromar

Editor: Nancy Miller
Production: Ingrid Luters
Cover art: Wendy Liddle

We acknowledge the financial support of the Government of Canada through the Book Publishing Industry Development Program (BPIDP) for our publishing activities.

Published simultaneously in Canada and the United States by

HANCOCK HOUSE PUBLISHERS LTD.
19313 Zero Avenue, Surrey, B.C. V4P 1M7
(604) 538-1114 Fax (604) 538-2262

HANCOCK HOUSE PUBLISHERS
1431 Harrison Avenue, Blaine, WA 98230-5005
(604) 538-1114 Fax (604) 538-2262
Web Site: www.hancockhouse.com *email:* sales@hancockhouse.com

Contents

Preface

For years I hid my writing underneath my socks and underwear in a drawer, and I never confessed to anyone that I was a poet! The growing popularity of cowboy and western folklife poetry continues to amaze me. In this era, it is both gratifying and surprising to see so many people who still appreciate the simple, honest values exemplified by the word "cowboy."

In addition to my own poems, I have included the works of a few special friends in this collection, primarily because their poems are not in print elsewhere and they should be available to the public.

W. H. (Bill) Stewart was perhaps the first real cowboy poet I ever met.

David Longworth is a cowboy poet and professional actor. Dave's poem "The Look" is about the passing of Mike Ferguson, longtime cowboss of Douglas Lake Cattle Co.—my first boss and mentor.

Kathy Schneider is a talented and up-and-coming poet, who is also my sister-in-law.

Gordon Wilson is a lifelong friend. Gordy and I have known each other since we were babies; he still ranches a few miles up the valley from me. His poem "Life of a Cowpony" may well be one of the all-time cowboy poetry classics.

I would like to dedicate this book to those old storytellers who left their mark on me, and my mom and dad 'cause it all started with them.

Meadow Muffins

A philosopher and cowboy,
born one step out of time,
tryin' to make
the world make sense,
in parables and rhyme.

To portray the western
way of life,
hoof, hide, hair and all,
and cover up with plain B.S.
The parts I can't recall!

Cowboy Poet?

My back's too sore for shoein' nags,
I've got water on the knee,
and no interest in most kinds of work
as you can plainly see.

My waste size keeps on sneakin' up
'til I'm now more round than tall.
I used to be an athlete,
now I don't do much at all.

But I can still tell a story
and swap lies all night long.
And suddenly that's respectable,
though it still seems kind of wrong.

All those years that ma cussed on me
for tellin' yarns and lies,
the time that I spent
dodging work, inventing alibis...

Who knew that I was in training,
just preparing for the time
when any B.S. artist can be a star
if he can make those damn lies
rhyme!

To Butcher a Rose

As a scientific dissection
mars the beauty of a rose,
so doth the English lesson
rend asunder simple prose.

For poetry is passion,
be it anger, love or pain;
the beauty of midsummer starlight,
or the smell of a sweet spring rain.

Let no scholarly pontification
render my rhymes stiff and cold,
as generations of "educators"
have done to the bards of old.

Poetry is passion—
if you teach it, do it right,
lest you douse poor Dylan's candle
or dim fair Juliet's light.

The Man My Sister Married

by Kathy Schneider

I remember the first time we met him
this beau that she had brought to the house,
she had given us an early warning
we never dreamed he would become her spouse.
He wasn't too tall but neither was she
and his hat was as wide as his shoulders,
there were specs on his nose and a duster beneath
and his swaggerin' walk shoulda told us.
The way of his gait was unfamiliar to us,
it was a sauntering rocking chair lope.
And the way that he spoke had a southern twang
and he answered with a yep and a nope.
He didn't speak too much, he was quiet and shy
with his lips always full of chew,
where we had come from this sort of thing
was something you just didn't do.
But he won all our hearts and nuptials took place
and he behaved like a gentle cowboy,
he was always polite and careful with drink
till a relative cracked through his ploy.
It was a hot summer night, the celebrating was high
and his tongue slowly greased with the liquor,
the stories he told kept us laughin' all night
'bout swattin' balls on a green, couldn't figure.
It was a night we remember and chuckle about
when his true self was finally revealed,
thank God we now know what he's really like,
this jokester he tried to conceal.

But you know this guy is full of surprises
and he's nothing like his appearance would seem,
'cause this retired old rodeo cowboy
has made reality out of his dreams.
He took some words and he made up his prose
that give enjoyment to all those that hear,
and the oils that he mixes come out as life
a pleasure to each one who peers.
He inspires those with a similar craft
to "keep dreamin' and don't
lose your goal,
'cause the words that you
write and the pictures
you paint
come from some-
where inside of your
soul."
We're proud of this
man and the art he's
created,
this farmer who's
humble at heart,
my brother-in-law,
this is Mikey
he always has a
story to start.

The Westerner

by David Longworth

I am a Westerner, born in Manitoba,
　　the heart of the land.
The hard grass prairie of Saskatchewan
　　is where I learned to stand
And ride beneath the bell-jar sky,
With the sun giving life then scorching dry.
I have served in the ranks of the reapers,
　　sending bread to our nation's homes
And move the cattle to market,
　　to build muscle on our children's bones.
I have fished in the Fraser for salmon
　　in British Columbia's storms.
Trod her forests and cut her timber
　　to make houses safe and warm.
I've been alone with the wind
　　on a rolling Alberta hill,
Been eagle high on a rocky divide
　　and felt part of a great divine will.
This proud land is living, it never stops giving.
　　it is a gift I ever shall honor
And treat with respect, not needless neglect,
　　in my brief passage on her.
So, I'll ride with full chest and take every test,
And praise the Creator for this blessed West.
I am a Westerner!

Keep the West Alive

Born a hundred years too late,
I've often heard that phrase.
A cowboy, in the space age,
out of step with modern ways.

Still pullin' calves in springtime,
and tryin' to save them all!
Makin' hay in the summer heat,
and roundups in the fall.

There's a natural rhythm
to a rancher's work—
checkin' cows or fixin' fence.
Doin' things that must be done,
it all makes perfect sense.

Sure the work is hard and endless,
but it's the kind that fits a man!
Where honest toil helps feed the world,
in tune with nature's plan.

Now at times I may get bothered
by all the modern strife—
Politicians, bankers and bureaucrats
that plague a rancher's life.

And I envy Charlie Russel,
John Chisholm and Goodnight.
But if all of us had lived back then....
Who would keep up the fight?

Sure I've missed the days of open range
and those big longhorn cattle drives,
But someone has to
pick up the reins,
and keep the west
ALIVE!

March Nights

Cold and snow
that won't let go,
and the calves
are coming fast.

If you doze off and miss one...
his first night is his last!

It's an unforgiving way of life
for those tied to the land.
And sleepless nights
are just one cost
of runnin' your own "brand."

You know spring will come,
it always does,
the grass will soon be green.
A warm breeze will play
through the leaves
in May,
But damn,
March nights
are mean!

A Late Spring

The south wind rattles the windows,
Another night without sleep.
The wind chimes tinkle like sleigh bells,
While my muses' company I keep.

The "endless winter"
Finally has ended.

But so has the whole month of March!
And the night sky over the Thompson
Is framed with a big chinook arch.

From November 'til the week just passed,
The fields were buried in snow.
So dry the mud and bring on the grass,
And blow you damn wind blow!

Friday, the Uh-Oh

Well I ain't superstitious myself,
it's like any other day.
But I remember when a spark
from the old John Deere
burned up fifty ton of hay!
And when I broke my arm,
the time I wrecked my truck,
just coincidence I'd say.
And I ain't superstitious,
but I'll stay close to home today!

Planning Ahead

*(Written for Steve and Kay Puhallo
on their fiftieth wedding anniversary.)*

Wedded bliss often goes amiss
over the little things in life.
And forgotten anniversaries
have brought many pairs to strife.
My parents dodged this hazard,
by a simple twist of fate,
when they began their life together
in nineteen forty-eight.
That famous winter of endless snow,
when they hardly saw sunlight.
Except of course for Ground Hog Day,
that one dawned clear and bright!
So through fifty years of marriage
no one forgot their date...
'Cause it was the day after
they shot the groundhog,
in nineteen forty-eight!

The Price of Respectability

Out in the wild Chilcotin
lives a man named "Chilco Choate,"
Grizzled old guide and mountain man
and writer of some note.
This longtime mountain wild man
of late has grown quite tame,
So when they announced all these new gun laws
he decided to play their game.
Only man west of the Fraser
to lock his guns and ammo up tight.
He nearly paid a horrible price
on a moonless summer night.
In that little wilderness cabin
the old gent lives alone
A good day's ride from the nearest ranch,
where roads are still unknown.
It was late on in the evening,
the old boy was about to turn in.
When suddenly on his tiny porch
there arose an awful din.
Of course, for him the sound was muted
with his hearing aid turned down,
But he thought he better take a peek
as he went to the door with a frown.
He barely got to unlatch the door
when it was blasted open wide
And two critters locked in mortal combat
tumbled right inside!

There he was defenceless,
pinned against the wall,
as a cougar and his old hound dog
fought a free for all.
He'd have dearly liked to help the dog
and relieve his desperate plight.
But on the north side of the livingroom
were his rifles, locked up tight!
He followed the law to the letter,
of that you can be sure.
'Cause in a cabinet on the southern wall
his bullets were secure!
Around and round the livingroom
the dog and wildcat went.
An' old Choate couldn't do a blessed thing
but cuss the government.

Sasquatch Hunt

There's strange critters in them mountains
and I know of which I speak,
for I saw the track of Bigfoot
in the sand by Pincher Creek.

It's late on in the evening
I'm feeling brave and strong.
'Cause with the aid of a setting sun
my shadow's twelve feet long.

Working along the creek bank
I'm hot upon the trail.
At the thought of what may lie ahead,
my courage starts to fail.

But now my tale ends in confusion.
For though a Sasquatch did I seek,
what I found was Terri Mason
coolin' her feet off in the creek!

Midnight Revelation

A million tiny points of light
thrown across a moonless sky.
On an ink black autumn night,
there's only God and I.

Such solitude and peace
and splendor spread on high—
those twinkling lights from so far away,
a feast for soul and eye.

Beneath such awesome beauty
on a moonless autumn night,
a man feels small and humble
amazed at all within my sight.

All doubts and cares are swept away
and all the world is right,
as I gaze into the face of God
on a moonless autumn night.

The Armchair Cowboy

by Kathy Schneider

He climbed up on the sofa arm
a little boy of only three,
dressed like a little cowboy
his show was on TV.
With a cowboy hat upon his head
and his holster by his side,
a rope was gripped on tightly
he was ready for his ride.
He would kick that armchair pony
chasing bandits all the way,
or maybe it was Indians,
can't remember to this day.
He hooted and he hollered
and he yipped to a table cow
saying, "Come on little doggie,
get a move on, hurry now."
And when his play was over
his lunch he'd run to see,
and then this tired little cowboy
slept upon his momma's knee.

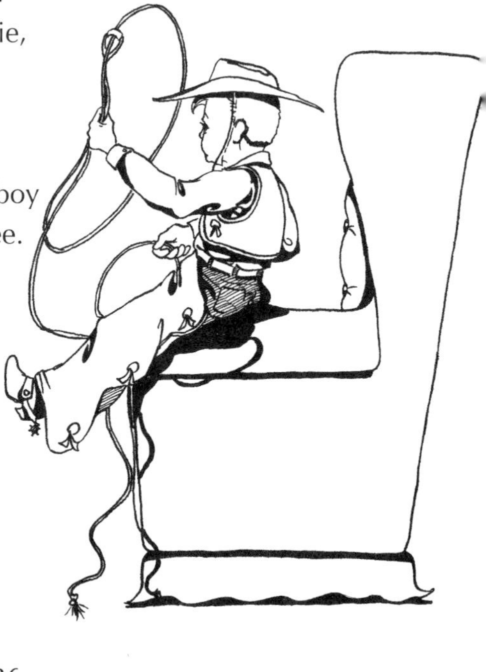

Signs of....Are You Sure This Is February

My pickup truck is still caked with mud,
but the feed ground's drying fast.
The ice is off the river
and two brave robins just flew past.
It's been an easy year for calving,
we've hardly seen the vet.
Though a little caution is advised,
winter ain't over yet.
Don't you remember last year?
And twenty-five below
dragging calves with frozen ears
through a foot of crusted snow?
But lets hope nature's signs don't lie
and we're done with winter's cares,
'cause all the geese I've seen this week
were flyin' round in pairs.

Canada Goosed

Target Farmers Unlimited,
those well-heeled urban cats
who masquerade as environmentalists
while altering habitats.

A grassy marsh or mallard pond
is of no use to them.
So if they can't build a dam to flood it,
they'll fill the whole thing in.

Curlews, rails or falcons
don't figure in their schemes
of megaprojects, media hype
and political pipe dreams.

With money rollin' in
from shotgun hunter fees,
they rearrange the wetlands
in the manner that they please.

Little creeks through peat bogs,
with their tiny ponds and swamps,
don't produce the "proper fowl,"
to meet a hunter's wants.

They'll dam that creek and make a lake,
so the geese will then move in.
And pickins for the smaller birds
will soon get pretty thin!

This environmental prejudice
confused me for a bit.
But I guess the boys that pay the bills
need a target they can hit.

A Ranch Wife's Advice
(Overheard at a branding party)

"Wrangler butts??!!
Little girl, you're nuts!"
(The ranch wife was disgusted)
"Them rodeo hands might have nice cans,
but looks ain't to be trusted."

"If you like the western way of life,
and seek a cowboy
for your mate,
you can overlook nearly any vice
if the man can hang a gate."

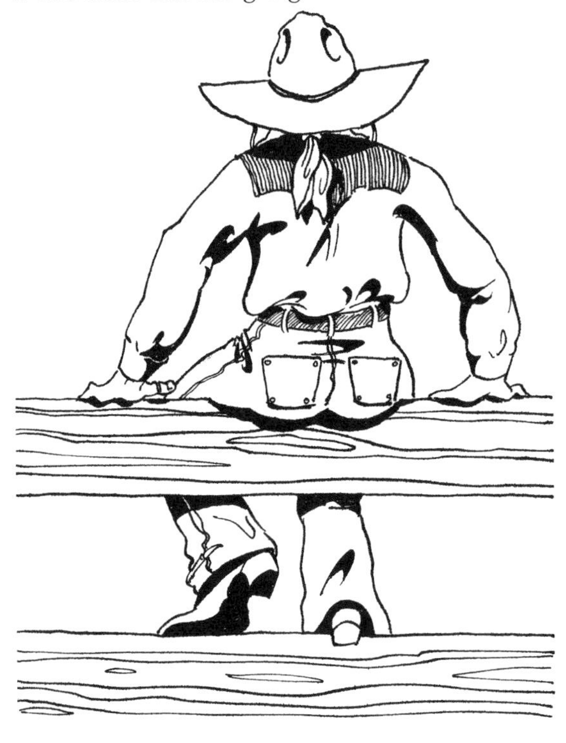

The Valley

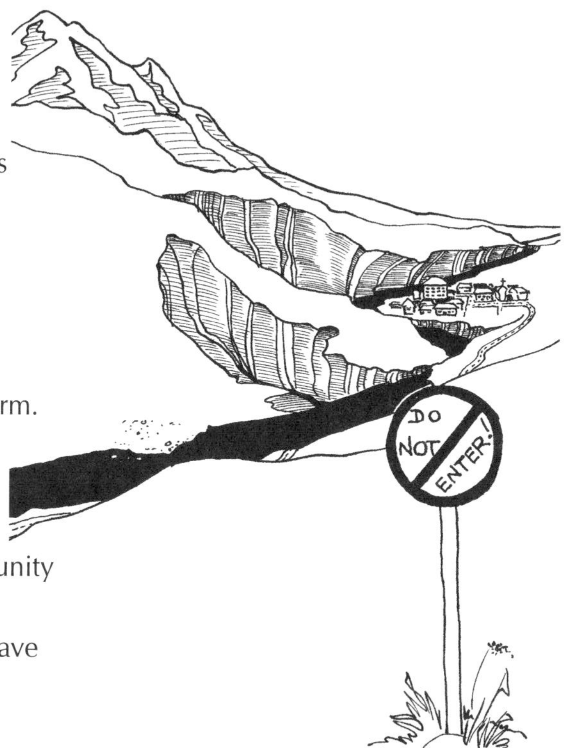

The glaciers and rivers
carved this place
with guidance divine
and a touch of grace.

That river now winds
through village and farm.
A vale of tranquility,
beauty and charm.

Here a diverse community
works hand in hand,
knowing all that we have
we owe to the land.

Here folks have chosen
the rural life
and little towns
free of urban strife.

To all of the schemers
who'd bring progress our way:
Our valley's just fine,
so please stay away!

A Kaleidoscope of Time

by W. H. Stewart

I wandered to a mountain top some fifty years ago,
To gaze at distant snow-clad peaks and a river far below.
Fringed by farms of varied hue, a patchwork of brown and
green,
This against the snow-capped peaks created a memorable scene.

My viewpoint was a parklike spot, a few trees and grass profuse.
The scars of a fire marked many a tree and the grass
showed wildlife use.
And sprouting from the forest floor, conifer seedlings
seeking the sun,
A lesson to the observant that nature's work is never done.

My mind retained that scene as thru' life I made my way,
Until at last I was privileged to return there one day.
But alas! A curtain had been drawn, there was no scene,
No grass, no wildlife trails, just a forest green.

A young forest too dense, striving for space and light,
It seemed there could be no winner in such a fight.
Refereed by a man who in his wisdom made it a rule
That fire was not suitable as a management tool.

I chanced again to pass that way not many moons ago
To view the evidence of nature deciding what would grow.
A deadened tangle of skeletons—denuded, rotting and falling—
Nature had ordered her insect army to move and do
her calling.

It was not a waste, perhaps, the soil will be enhanced.
A new forest is sitting in the wings with many other plants.
And Nature will continue, though we strive to change her way,
To manage this land from year to year and a little every day.

But if headstrong man had thinned those trees,
Nature could have provided much more to the economy,
With grass for ungulates and logs for mills,
A partnership for the good of all and dollars to jingle the tills.

I pondered these thoughts as I searched for a hole
Through the jungle confronting my aged body and soul.
And then through those denuded trees, Behold!
The river, the snowcaps, as I remembered from long ago.

Poor Choices

As his lifeblood stains
the crusted snow,
he can't dig through
to reach them,
but he can hear the mice below.

The farmyard wasn't his first choice,
where dogs and shotguns wait.
But a starving mate and pups at home
have sealed the coyote's fate.

Whose Lies?

The history of the west
is oft told upside down.
'Cause the folks who got to tell the tale
were the last to come around.

So gather up the old one's tales
and try to write them down.
Seek out the lore and legends
that still are passed around.

I've searched the dusty archives
and read the ancient lies
that have become our history,
but let me set you wise.

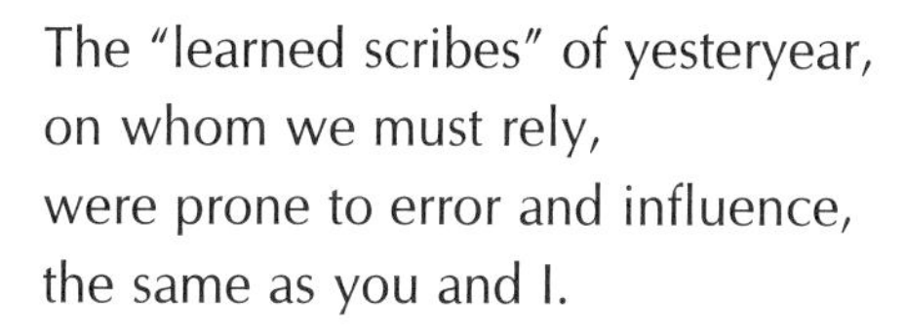

The "learned scribes" of yesteryear,
on whom we must rely,
were prone to error and influence,
the same as you and I.

The wild and wooly campfire tales
he learned at grandpap's knee,
passed on now through ancient lips.
Now folks, that's history!

May First

Well I rototilled the garden
and finally mowed the lawn,
pulled the hoses from the shed
and turned the water on.

We're branding calves this weekend,
I've turned the yearlings out on grass,
the river's brown and muddy
and the water's rising fast.

I've got a mile of fence to build
and ten acres left to plow.
It seems the chores I've been puttin' off
all need doin' now!

But that work will keep a little while,
as we stroll the river's rim
and watch a clutch of baby geese
go out for their first swim.

Lies, Legends and Road Apples

From timothy to apples,
it seems a horse's favorite feeds
all have one thing in common,
they've all got
little seeds.

And everywhere man travels
the horse, of course,
has gone.
And the seeds of
all its favorite feeds,
they kind of spread along.

Road apples
are a marvelous thing
when you stop
to think of it.
Perhaps even the legend
of Johnny Appleseed was
the result of plain horse----!

Just a Yodelin' Cowboy

I dreamed of being a cowboy star
up on that silver screen—
a yodeling singing ranger,
like Roy and Rex and Gene.
But I couldn't learn to yodel,
no matter how I tried.
Every time I air my tonsils out
it sounds like something died!

Ode to a Mule

Stubbornness
by some is thought
with strength
to be entwined.

But oft as not,
'tis just the mask
that hides
a narrow mind!

Still Kickin'

An old cowboy might moan
and whine
and cuss about his age.
The infirmities that sneak up
on you
each time life turns a page.

Yup gettin' older is a bitch,
that much I'll have to give.
But, all things being equal,
it beats the alternative!

Winter Sports

The Arctic front blew in today,
so cold your breath comes short.
It's time for me to partake once more
in my favorite winter sport.
Concentration is the key;
I work hard at this thing,
as I curl up in my easy chair
and dream of distant spring.

Hay Fever

So I work a while, then sneeze a while,
and struggle through the day.
A farmer blessed with allergies
has no fun making hay.
I wear a mask while baling
to filter out the dust.
Nose spray, antihistamines
and eye drops are a must.
Why I endure this misery
is hard for some to see.
To me it's just the interest
on the price of being me.
So I sneeze a while, then work a while,
and don't let it get me down.
I'll take the good with the bad
'cause I just can't live in town!

Calving Time

January has slipped away,
there's warmth now in the sun.
And along the ol' North Thompson,
calving time's begun.

Clean bedding hauled and put in place
to keep those babies dry.
Vet supplies and calf jacks are ready,
standing by.

While the Nicola Valley cowboy
sharp shoes his favorite horse,
we get ready for calving
with new "gumboots" of course.

Ode to McQueen Creek

It seemed a simple thing to me
that little creeks have the right to be.

It's endured more than a century of
diversions, dams and fills,
and McQueen Creek still
seeks a path
to the river from the hills.

Around eighteen sixty the
Hudson's Bay
first diverted the stream to water
an orchard and vegetable farm.
Progress, so it would seem...

The channel long filled,
the willows ripped out,
that used to line this little
creek's course.
The degraded stream had
all but dried up.
The farmers had found a new source.

But the dry years passed by and a wet cycle came.
The little creek roared back to life.
The "experts" all claimed,
"It's not really a creek,
ground water's the cause of your strife!"

Three years have passed since
McQueen Creek's return
first flooded basements and field.
And if water management folks have a plan,
well, at best, it ain't been revealed.

I've redug the channel across our land
to set McQueen Creek free.
But, alas, there's still,
ten miles upstream,
clogged with bureaucracy!

Schedules

I greased the swather and got ready to hay,
then thought I'd wait another day.
It clouded up and threatened to rain,
so I put the swather away again.
This went on for more than a week—
Storm clouds and I playing hide and seek.

The cattleman's convention was another fine ruse
to hold off on hayin', I don't need much excuse.
So I headed for town to swap stories and lies,
while that ol' haymaker shone through azure blue skies!
I've stalled off my hayin' as long as I dare,
Alberta's callin', in two weeks I'll be there.

So now, rain or shine, I'll cut hay this week,
'cause she's got to be done before I hit Pincher Creek.
Farmers and poets that wear the same hide
know what is important and what to let slide.
And if the weather socks in and the hay just won't dry,
well, it won't be the first time we made bales in July!

What Next?

Blew a tire on the trailer
with a load of heifers on.
Told the wife I'd be home by dark
when I left the house at dawn.
A heavy pull up from Little Fort,
the old truck's runnin' hot.
It starts to rain, as I crest the hill,
it starts to rain a lot!
For an hour I faced the driving rain,
then it finally let up some.
And out of the mist straight ahead...
Where did that deer come from?
I dodged him once, then he turned back
and tried to cross again.
He smashed my mirror then jumped the fence
and disappeared into the rain.

I left the pavement at Hanceville,
thirty miles left to travel.
That big hill above the Chilco Ranch
could use a little gravel.
Almost made it, I used the crowd gate in trailer
to shift more weight onto my truck,
And with the front wheels nearly off the ground,
proceeded through the muck!
Unloaded at the twilight ranch,
caught some zees then headed home.
Battery went dead in 100 Mile,
the voltage regulators blown.

Thirty-five bucks and a bit of wire
and I'm on my way again.
"You can't get parts on Canada Day,
but this might just get you in."
The old truck kept together
thanks to luck and bailing wire.
And my journey ended as it began,
I blew another tire!

Canada Day?

It's Dominion Day in the Great White North,
at least that's what it used to be
'til some political hack changed the name
just to cause confusion for me.
Canada Day would be better they'd say,
more politically correct.
A name devoid of any meaning
with no message to suspect.
No words that hint of dominance
can be used in this great land,
for it might alarm our neighbors to the south
and reveal our master plan!
We lead the world in so many ways,
and have for quite awhile,
and they hardly notice our dominance,
'cause we do it "Canadian" style.

El Niño

The image of a cozy rural home
nestled in the trees
is somewhat less than calming
in summers such as these.

The undergrowth and whispering pines
that gave our home such grace,
have now become a tinder box
through which the flames may race.

For those who keep their rural roots
and let the rat race pass them by
all share the risk and know the dread
when the forest gets too dry.

The lawn I always hate to mow,
the shade I used to prize—
now I wish I'd cut those darn trees down
and the lawn was twice its size!

Conservation?

Fuzzy Wuzzy was a bear
that wandered into town.
And just because he was a bear,
they shot poor Fuzzy down.

Now, I ain't much on preachin'
and I've shot a bear or two,
But the slaughter goin' on this year
disgusts me through and through.

Fifty-eight in Kamloops
have been sacrificed this summer.
'Cause when they're budget cutting,
a bear's life is a bummer.

Of course the gunner's motives
are well beyond reproach.
'Cause there'll be no illegal hunting
when there's nothing left to poach!

The gall bladder and bear parts trade
will be halted in a flash
as our "conservation officers"
keep conserving the government's cash!

The Look

by David Longworth

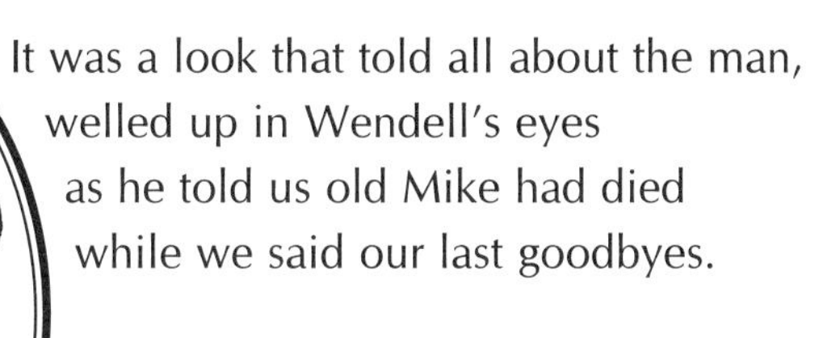

It was a look that told all about the man,
welled up in Wendell's eyes
as he told us old Mike had died
while we said our last goodbyes.

He said, "I'm happy about us winnin',
but there's a kind of sadness too."
Mike was the cowboss for forty-five years,
there before most of us were new.

T-Bow said, "We're going to miss him for sure,
in a lot of different ways.
That knee operation was to make things better.
He was supposed to come home today."

We flowed away from the arena,
streamlined trailers and dust and lights.
And I felt for the hands of the one-eleven
and the man they'd lost that night.

Mike Ferguson was a top hand,
a friend, a mentor and boss.
Now his ride had reached the river,
and today was his time to cross.

But boys, he'll never reach the Home Ranch,
he'll still ride those ranges each day.
'Cause Mike knew that Heaven's not far from the Douglas,
it's only fifteen hands away.

Shadow Camp

I often camp in that twilight world
between conscious thought and dreams—
a realm of ghostly images,
confusing, mixed up themes.

Oft times in this shadow world
I see faces from the past—
forgotten heroes and legends
I gaze upon at last.

Around a ghostly campfire
they stop to pass the time—
with tales of when the west was wild
and they were in their prime.

Gokleya and Chief Joseph,
Tom Horn and Russel too,
have visited my dreamscape camp
and shared their points of view
Imagination, dreams or madness,
I'll leave that up to you.
But each night around my "campfire"
are ghosts of men I never knew...

Adios John

(In memory of John Anderson)

The wind ripples the bunch grass
at the closing of the day.
The soul of a footloose cowboy
passes on his way.
His troubles long forgotten,
he's driftin' on with ease,
'cause the Lord made the cowboy
brother to the breeze.

A kindred soul and old friend
departed and passed on,
and a cowboy from top to bottom
was my old pal John.

A heart too big
and a soul too free,
a city man
he could never be.

Now his soul has crossed
that last divide
to where men like
Will James and Russel ride.

When I see the wind in the grass,
as it ripples along,
I'll just tip my hat
and say Adios John.

Jack's Favorite Song

The preacher who called him a pioneer
knew nothing of his past.
A reckless soul who'd wandered the west,
from his first day to his last.

They sang all the standard hymns
about eternal peace and joy.
And none of them knew
that his favorite tune was
"That Wild Colonial Boy."

The nurse from the hospital,
a grandnephew and niece or two
paid their last respects
to a man they never knew.
Oh they were familiar
with the old gentleman,
but they could not see inside.
For in that shell still dwelled a man
who was born to hunt and ride.

Yeah, they sent him off
with the standard hymns
about eternal peace and joy.
But can anyone here
remember the tune
to "That Wild Colonial Boy"?

A Pioneer

by W. H. Stewart

I've survived on this land for a hundred years or so,
I've seen it in the summer heat and winters deep
with snow,
My roots run deep and I'm supposed to be part of
the past.
But I'm growing tired, one day soon will be my last.
My body's badly twisted, there are scars on my hide.
The thatch is gone from my top, where it once grew
with pride.
My summer clothes are thinner now, my limbs are raw
and sore,
My veins do not deploy my blood, as in days of yore.
I once stood erect and tall, ready for any storm or strife,
Proud as I grew and prepared to be part of any ongoing
life,
Ready to nurture other living souls and share with
affection
Many visitors from afar in need of care and protection.
Those days are gone, just a memory soon to end,
For I have grown brittle and can no longer bend.
A good strong wind shall upset me and lay me on
the ground,
And folks will say, "Too bad, it used to be the finest
tree around."

Life of a Cowpony

by Gordon Wilson

Two horses were standing by a gate,
one was there to learn his fate.
The other said, "Now why are you here?
Tell the truth now, no bum steer.

"Tell me your life, lets hear it all,
from spring to spring, and fall to fall.
From the days of your youth till the very end,
take your time we have hours to spend."

"Well, I was born in the hills running free,
just an old coyote, my momma and me.
It was like that for nigh on two years,
then I met man and terrible fear.

"They marked my hide and used a sharp knife,
I knew for sure it was the end of my life.
I kicked and squealed my anger that day,
then they said, 'You're here to stay.'

"They roped my neck and snubbed me tight,
my wind was cut off, so I couldn't fight.
They covered my eyes with a big old sack,
cinched on a saddle and pulled out the slack.

"Then a man climbed on my back,
he jerked off the blind and gave me slack.
I was free at last, I was leaving there,
but that man on my back was stuck like hair.

"I bogged my head and started to pop,
then I flattened out and spun like a top.
I bucked and jumped till I was dead on my feet,
I'd been ridden to the end by a man named Pete.

"He stepped to the ground and said,'I like him fine,
I think I'll make this pony mine,
I'll work this horse, I'll take my time,
in a month or two he'll turn on a dime.'

"Well Pete was okay, he wasn't that bad,
my momma was gone, he was all that I had.
So we formed a bond as time went on,
I don't know where all the time has gone.

"He would always use me when the going got rough,
then he would brag to the boys about my 'extra stuff'.
He would tell them how I could travel in the open,
how I could sure work a rope when a cow needed doping.

"Where on earth did all those good years go?
In no time at all my age started to show.
My shoulders got stiff, I wasn't that sound,
I couldn't be trusted on rough ground.

"Then one day Pete brought me from my pen,
said, 'Old boy, you're going back to work again.
This here job will suit you just fine,
teach him to ride, this son of mine.'

"Well that little boy was one dumb pup,
he didn't know which end was up,
Just move real slow, and that was all,
one quick turn and sonny would fall.

"He'd hit the ground and start to cry,
then he'd climb back on for another try.
He got to riding better each day,
once he was on he was there to stay.

"I remember once I had to give him a toss,
some girls were there, he was showing off.
I bogged my head and really cut loose,
he flew through the air like an old goose.

"He came off the ground spitting blood and dirt,
his hat was all bent, he'd torn his shirt.
He was hunting a rock, he sure was mad,
but just in time, here come his dad.

"He said, 'Settle down son, I watched it all,
and I have to say you deserved that fall.
He was just letting you know the only way he can,
it's time for you to grow up, now be a man.'

"Well, from that day on I was ridden no more,
now I was all stove up and doing real poor.
I couldn't eat oats, I was long in the tooth,
my life was about over, I knew it for truth.

"Then yesterday I lay down for a nap,
when I went to get up I heard something snap.
Pete packed me some water, some grain and hay,
but we both knew I was down to stay.

"His wife asked if she should call the vet,
the look in Pete's eyes I'll never forget.
'There's nothing to do, what's done is done,
go back to the house, I'll get the gun.'

"He said I really hate to do this to you,
cause you were the best through and through.
I wouldn't have traded you for ten
of the best horses in any man's pen.

"So that was the end of my days
with that old cowboy and his funny ways.
Now I know what it's like to die,
and now I know that cowboys do cry.

"So now I've come to see you my maker,
give it to me straight, I can take her.
I'm all worn out, I'm broken and old,
do I still get to pass through your gate of gold?"

"I'm stepping aside, your way is clear,
your green pastures await not far from here.
For I've heard your story, you're not a phoney,
you've earned that distinguished title 'Cowpony'."

P.S.
Pete never went back home that night,
he went to a bar and started a fight.
Wasn't long till he landed in jail,
and had to call his wife to post bail.

She didn't get mad or give him hell,
cause she knew only too well.
Only a lucky cowboy in his life
is entitled to one "good" horse, dog and wife.